STEP-by-STEP

GEOGRAPHY

Towns and Cities

Patience Coster

Illustrated by Shirley Bellwood
and Raymond Turvey

CHILDREN'S PRESS®

A Division of Grolier Publishing

NEW YORK • LONDON • HONG KONG • SYDNEY
DANBURY, CONNECTICUT

© 1997 Franklin Watts

American Edition 1998 by
Children's Press
A Division of Grolier Publishing Co., Inc
Sherman Turnpike
Danbury, Connecticut 06813

Library of Congress Cataloging-in-Publication Data
Coster, Patience.
Towns and cities/Patience Coster; illustrated by Shirley Bellwood and Raymond Turvey.--1st American ed.
p. cm. --(Step-by-step geography)   Includes index.
Summary; The story of the development of cities and towns around the world including their
buildings, neighborhoods, transportation systems, recreational activities, problems, and people.
ISBN 0-516-20355-X
1. Cities and towns--Juvenile literature. [1. Cities and towns.] I. Bellwood, Shirley, ill.
II. Turvey, Raymond, ill. III. Title. IV. Series.
HT152.C67   1998
307.76--dc21   97-16182   CIP   AC

Printed in Dubai

Planning and production by The Creative Publishing Company
Design: Ian Winton
Consultant: Philip Steele

Photographs: Bruce Coleman: page 8, bottom, and page 25, top (Thomas Buchholz);
Mary Evans Picture Library: page 8, top; Robert Harding Picture Library: page 7 (Rolf Richardson),
page 10 (Walter Rawlings), page 18, page 20 (Adina Tovy), page 21, bottom, page 26; Hutchison Library:
page 11, page 21, top (Philip Wolmuth); Image Bank: cover (Steve Dunwell), page 5, top (Romilly Lockyer),
page 28, top (Yat Nin Chan); Tony Stone Worldwide: page 5, bottom (Mark Segal), page 9 (Bill Pogue),
page 16 (David Hanson), page 25, bottom (Paul Chesley), page 29 (Geoff Johnson), page 30 (Jean Pragen),
page 31; ZEFA: page 19, page 23, page 27, page 28, bottom (Richard).

Contents

Where People Live

Where do you live? If there are just a few houses, it is a village. If there are lots of houses and stores, it is a town. If the town is very big or important, it is called a city.

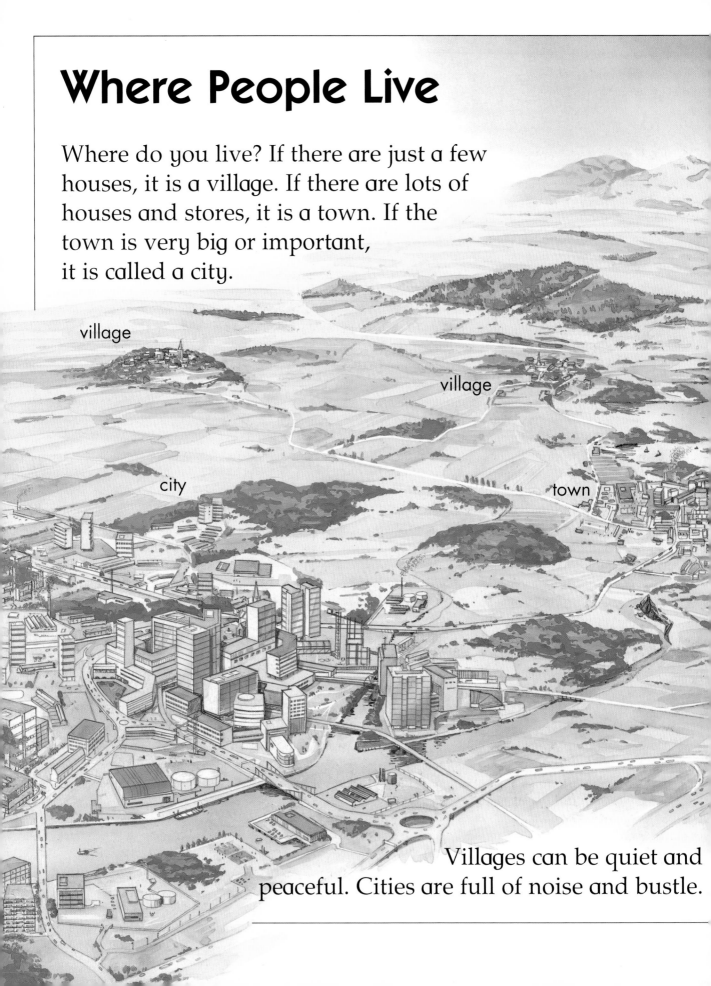

village

village

city

town

Villages can be quiet and peaceful. Cities are full of noise and bustle.

Most people in the world live in towns and cities. This is Sarlat, a small town in France. Many of the buildings here date back hundreds of years. The houses are no more than four **stories** high.

This is Chicago in the United States of America. Chicago is a large city with many tall, modern buildings called skyscrapers.

The First Towns

Long ago, people did not live in one place.
They wandered in search of food. Once they started
to tame animals and grow crops, people began to settle
in villages. The first towns grew up
about 10,000 years ago.

Towns grew up along trade routes. In these centers, people
could sell goods such as grain, animals, spices, and gold.

Large ports grew up on sea routes, and inland cities grew up along **caravan** routes. Damascus in Syria is an important city that began as a small trading post on a caravan route.

If you visit an ancient town today you will find many of the oldest buildings, like churches and castles, in the center. There may also be narrow streets, made before cars were invented.

When Towns Grew Bigger

About two hundred years ago, cities began to grow and grow. Big factories were built. People poured in from the countryside looking for work.

Hong Kong, pictured below, used to be a fishing village. Today it is a large, crowded port, one of the busiest cities in East Asia.

Many people decided to live in or near the growing cities. They could travel to town quickly and easily on the new railroads and roads. Houses were built in the surrounding countryside. These areas were called the suburbs. People could **commute** from the suburbs to work in towns and cities.

People in Towns and Cities

Many people have lived in towns and cities all their lives. Others move there in search of work, education, or excitement.

Sometimes there is not enough work or housing to go around. If people can't find jobs, life can be hard. In many cities there are people without jobs or homes.

When so many people want homes, space becomes valuable. In cities, people usually live quite close to one another. City houses are often joined together in a **terrace**. There may be some **detached** homes, but many houses are divided into apartments. There are also **bungalows** and **high-rise buildings**.

Cities of the World

Many of the world's important cities have famous landmarks, such as churches, skyscrapers, and statues.

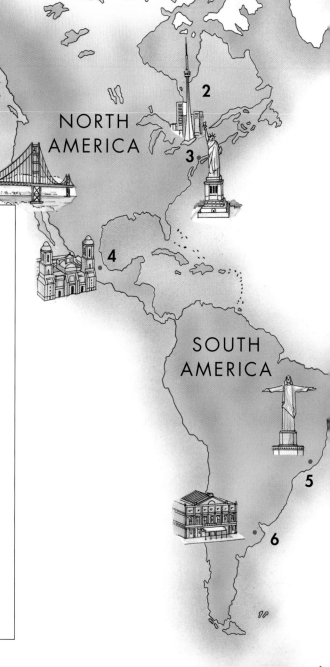

NORTH AMERICA

SOUTH AMERICA

1

2

3

4

5

6

MAKE A TOURISM POSTER

Make a poster advertising your town. Does it have a church, a museum, a theater? Did someone famous grow up there? Does it have an annual festival or carnival? What other things do you think tourists might like to visit in your town?

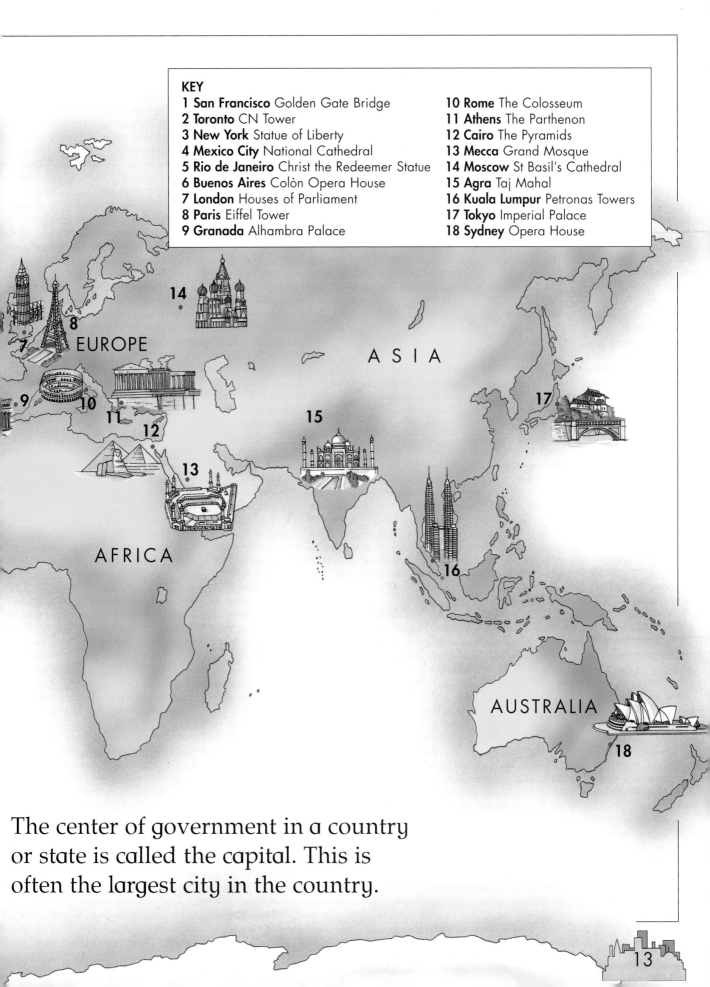

KEY

1 **San Francisco** Golden Gate Bridge
2 **Toronto** CN Tower
3 **New York** Statue of Liberty
4 **Mexico City** National Cathedral
5 **Rio de Janeiro** Christ the Redeemer Statue
6 **Buenos Aires** Colòn Opera House
7 **London** Houses of Parliament
8 **Paris** Eiffel Tower
9 **Granada** Alhambra Palace

10 **Rome** The Colosseum
11 **Athens** The Parthenon
12 **Cairo** The Pyramids
13 **Mecca** Grand Mosque
14 **Moscow** St Basil's Cathedral
15 **Agra** Taj Mahal
16 **Kuala Lumpur** Petronas Towers
17 **Tokyo** Imperial Palace
18 **Sydney** Opera House

EUROPE

ASIA

AFRICA

AUSTRALIA

The center of government in a country
or state is called the capital. This is
often the largest city in the country.

Who Runs Towns and Cities?

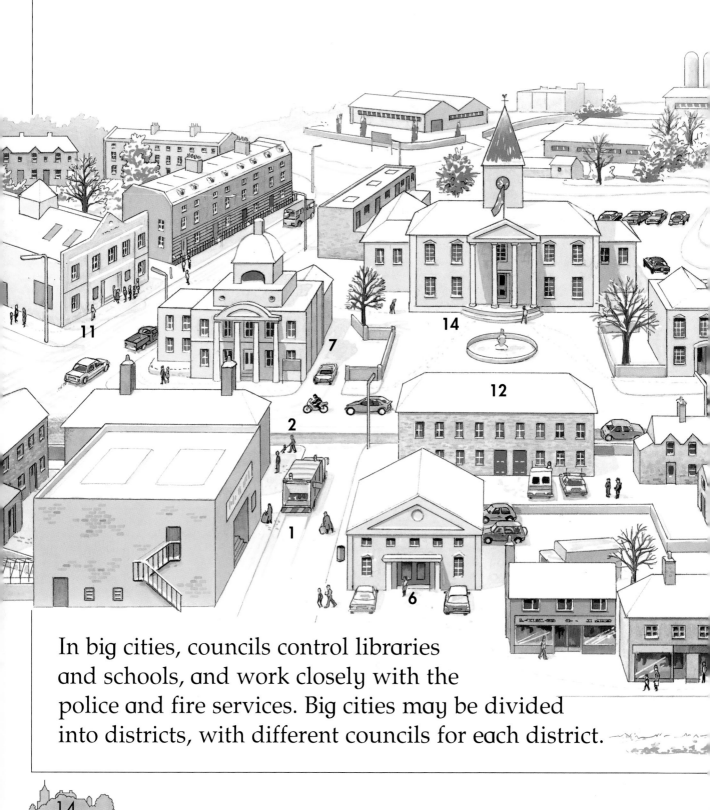

In big cities, councils control libraries
and schools, and work closely with the
police and fire services. Big cities may be divided
into districts, with different councils for each district.

The people in the town or city choose who will run the council in **elections**. The head of the council is called a mayor. The mayor and council members have regular meetings at which they discuss problems and hear the views of people living in the community.

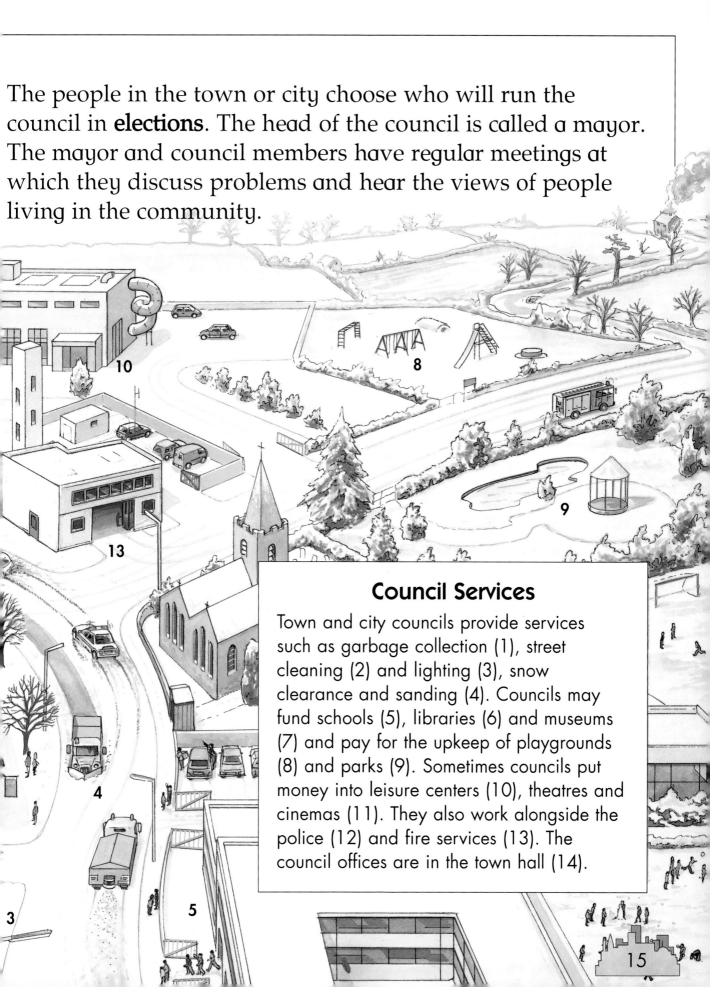

Council Services

Town and city councils provide services such as garbage collection (1), street cleaning (2) and lighting (3), snow clearance and sanding (4). Councils may fund schools (5), libraries (6) and museums (7) and pay for the upkeep of playgrounds (8) and parks (9). Sometimes councils put money into leisure centers (10), theatres and cinemas (11). They also work alongside the police (12) and fire services (13). The council offices are in the town hall (14).

Supplying a City

Where do the essential supplies of a city come from? How do food and water reach all the people that live there? Where do gas and electricity come from? The picture shows how these supplies are delivered to a city.

These wires carry messages by phone and fax.

Electricity is carried from a power station by cables. The cables are put underground when they reach the city.

Street Markets

This is a fruit and vegetable market in Goa, India. The produce is grown in the surrounding countryside and brought to town fresh every day.

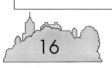

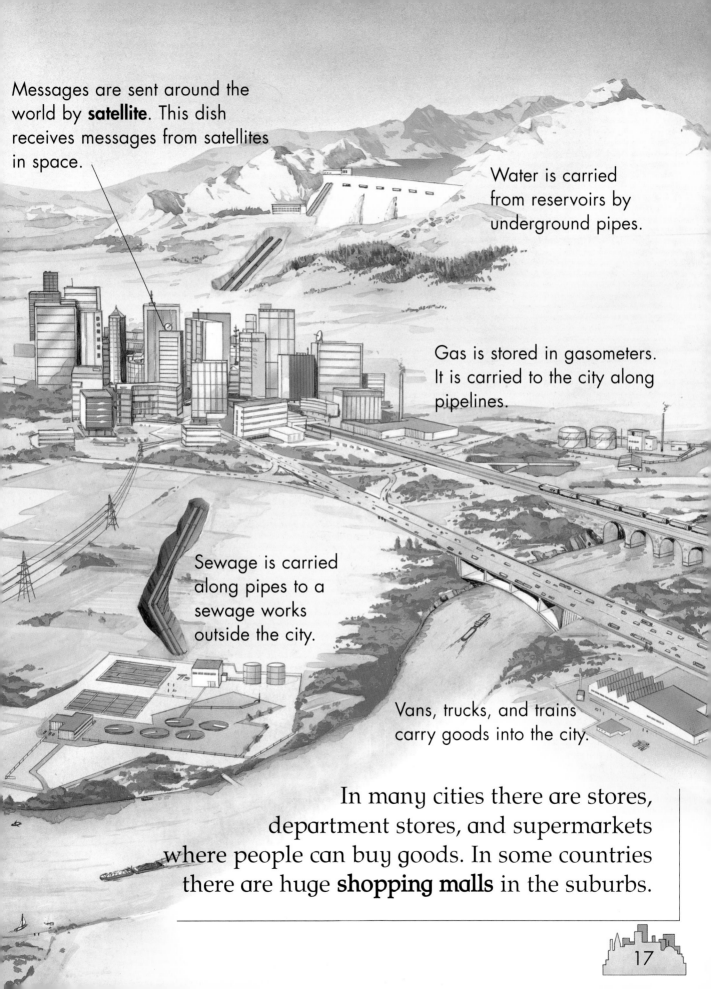

Messages are sent around the world by **satellite**. This dish receives messages from satellites in space.

Water is carried from reservoirs by underground pipes.

Gas is stored in gasometers. It is carried to the city along pipelines.

Sewage is carried along pipes to a sewage works outside the city.

Vans, trucks, and trains carry goods into the city.

In many cities there are stores, department stores, and supermarkets where people can buy goods. In some countries there are huge **shopping malls** in the suburbs.

Town and City Buildings

What do the buildings look like where you live? Are they old or modern, three-story houses or skyscrapers?

Cities usually contain a mixture of old and new buildings. Older buildings may be made of stone, brick, or wood. New buildings, like skyscrapers, are often made of concrete. Buildings are designed by **architects**, who choose which materials to use.

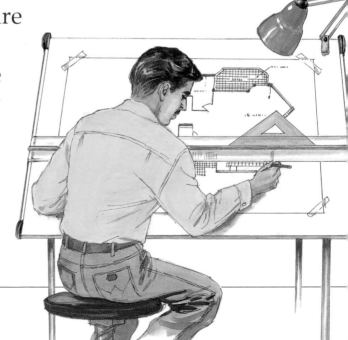

In many cities there are big skyscrapers. There was little room to build outwards, so people built upwards instead.

MAKE A SKYSCRAPER

1 Collect several cardboard boxes of different sizes. Glue them one on top of the other, with the larger boxes at the bottom and the smaller ones at the top.

2 Paint the stack of boxes grey. Paint windows and doors in black. How many levels high is your skyscraper?

Neighborhoods and Districts

Most cities have bustling centers, with offices where people work in all kinds of businesses.

Many cities also have distinct districts and neighborhoods. These may once have been separate villages which were swallowed up by the city as it grew.

Chinatown

In San Francisco, USA, people of Chinese origin live together in an area called Chinatown. Here many of the buildings are Chinese in style.

Some neighborhoods may be the home of people who originally came from another region or from overseas. These places still have their own character. The people living there often have their own customs, food, festivals, and carnivals. The photo above shows Notting Hill Carnival in London, England.

Transportation and Travel

In many towns and cities it is easy to walk from place to place. But sometimes you may need to take a bus, a train or subway, a car, or a taxi.

City traffic often gets stuck in jams. Roads and **monorail** tracks may have to be built over or under other roads. Subway trains carry passengers through the city quickly and easily. In some large cities, helicopters transport people to heliports in the center. Look at the picture. It shows city road and rail networks and different kinds of traffic.

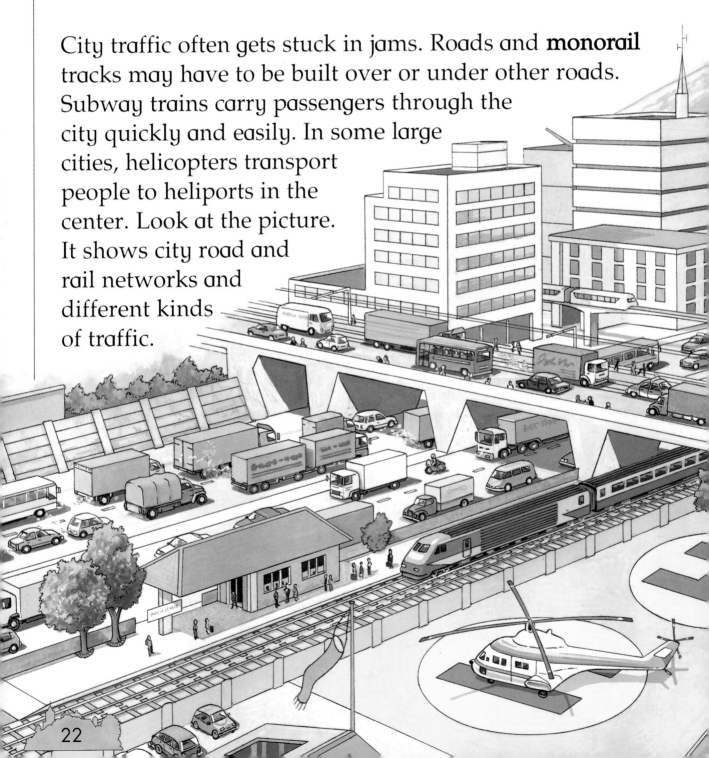

Streets of Water

There are no cars in the city of Venice in Italy. All the traffic travels by canal. People use waterbuses and **gondolas** to move themselves and their goods from one place to another.

Working in Towns and Cities

In towns and cities, people do lots of different jobs. Many people work in government offices. People also work in factories, offices, restaurants, banks, and hotels. They sell goods in stores, markets, and bazaars.

park keeper

office workers

postal worker

shop worker

taxi driver

Drivers are needed for the buses, taxis, and trains that move people around. Towns and cities also need postal workers, trash collectors, cleaners, police, ambulance and fire services.

The Rush Hour

In most towns and cities, some times of the day are busier than others. The busiest times are usually at the beginning and the end of the day, when people travel to and from work. These times are called "rush hours." This photo shows a crowded station at rush hour in Tokyo, the capital of Japan.

Having Fun in the City

Entertainment is an important part of city life. People enjoy themselves in cinemas, theaters, restaurants, clubs, art galleries, exhibition centers, sports stadiums, and concert halls. Tourists can visit famous sights.

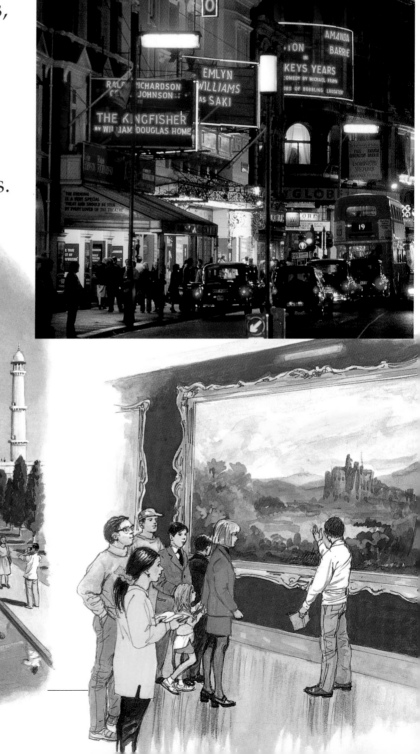

Parks and Gardens

Cities often have beautiful parks and gardens where people can stroll, picnic, and play games.

Major sporting events are usually held in cities. The Olympic Games are held in a different city every four years. In many towns and cities there are colleges that run evening classes, and sports centers where people can go to get all kinds of exercise.

Town and City Problems

Towns and cities are exciting and fun, but they have plenty of problems. They are crowded, and people create a lot of garbage. Sometimes this is hard to get rid of.

Exhaust fumes from cars, vans, and buses make the air unhealthy to breathe.

When cities are very overcrowded, people often cannot find work or homes. They may end up living in poor housing without proper services.

In some cities people are trying to improve life by banning cars and providing housing that people can afford. Factories are encouraged to produce less **pollution**, and to dispose of industrial waste safely.

A Clean City

In Reykjavík, the capital of Iceland, there is little air pollution because people don't burn fuel. The houses are heated by hot water from natural **springs** underneath the city.

Changing Towns and Cities

The first towns were not properly planned. They grew up in a fairly random way. In Prague in the Czech Republic, you can see a mix of old and new buildings and streets.

Prague is a beautiful city, but it is not a planned city. It has grown up gradually over the centuries.

Brasilia, the capital of Brazil, is a new, planned city. It has wide roads so that people can travel around easily by car. But new cities like this aren't always popular. Many people feel that older towns and cities have more character, and are livelier, friendlier places in which to live.

DESIGN A TOWN

Draw a plan of your ideal town. Would it be on a hill, by a river, or near the coast? Would it have lots of skyscrapers, older style buildings, or a mix of both? What services and facilities would you include?

Glossary

Architect A person whose job is to design buildings

Bungalow A single story house

Caravan A group of traders traveling together (especially across the desert in Asia and North Africa)

Community A group of people living in the same place

Commute To travel to and from daily work in the town or city

Detached home A house not joined to another on either side

Election The choice by voters of a person for office

Exhaust The used gases from a vehicle engine

Gondola A flat-bottomed boat with a high point at each end, used on canals in Venice, Italy

High-rise building A building with many stories

Monorail A railway running on a single rail

Pollution Land and water that has become dirty or harmful to human, animal, or plant life

Satellite A device rocketed into space to circle the Earth

Shopping mall An enclosed shopping center for pedestrians

Spring A flow of water from the ground

Story All that part of a building on the same floor

Terrace A row of houses joined together on either side

Index